It's Time
For a Spiritual Checkup

Is Your Thermometer Gauge
Hot, Cold or Luke Warm?

Frances Knight-Pinckney

WestBow
P R E S S
A DIVISION OF THOMAS NELSON

WestBow Press books may be ordered through booksellers or by contacting:

WestBow Press
A Division of Thomas Nelson
1663 Liberty Drive
Bloomington, IN 47403
www.westbowpress.com
1-(866) 928-1240

ISBN: 978-1-4908-0571-9 (sc)
ISBN: 978-1-4908-0572-6 (e)

Library of Congress Control Number: 2013915281

Printed in the United States of America.

WestBow Press rev. date: 8/28/2013

CONTENTS

DIVINE INSPIRATION

It's Time for a Spiritual Checkup

I was led to write this book while I was on my second 21-Day Daniel Fast in January 2008. I was watching a well-known pastor on television, and he asked, "What upsets you the most as a Christian?" He further stated that the area God is calling you into is an area you wish you could somehow change and one that you are extremely passionate about. Moreover, it is an area that you have been working in or around nearly all of your life. I pondered that question for a moment, and without a doubt, I knew this book had to be written. Not only am I extremely passionate about writing, but I am extremely passionate about bringing clarification through my writing. The Holy Spirit then led me to read notes I had written in my journal and sure enough, God's plan was already there for the writing of this book. It is amazing how God can move through fasting and praying.

You see, even as a young child, I always loved to write. I remember making up my own stories for my sister to read. Even to this day, my sister remembers this. As an adult, I still write in a journal. It is crucial to journal everything the Holy Spirit reveals to you, even if you think it is not of importance. You do this because it is rare that God shows you everything all at once. Journaling will allow you to go back and read what the Holy Spirit has revealed to you in the past. As you continue to journal exactly what the Holy Spirit allows you to hear or see, you will discover at the appointed time the whole piece of the puzzle. In other words, you will be able to see the complete picture that God intends for you to see.

As Christians begin to mature spiritually, their lifestyles should begin to reflect that of Jesus Christ. Consequently people should be able to distinguish Christians from non-Christians as their walks mature. As Christians begin to mature and express reverence for God through an intimate relationship with Him, their desire to walk away from sin and evil should increase. The Word of God says, "The fear of the Lord is to hate evil: pride, and arrogancy, and the evil way, and the forward mouth, do I hate" (Proverbs 8:13). As Christians we do not need to conform to the world but live lives that cause the world to conform to us. It's time for a spiritual checkup.

—Minister Frances Knight-Pinckney

ACKNOWLEDGMENTS

Firstly and lastly I want to acknowledge the Trinity—the Father, the Son, and the Holy Spirit. I thank You for leading me through, for seeing me through, and most importantly for carrying me through. I could stop right there because with those three you can't go wrong.

However, God has placed many special people in my life. I thank God for my church family, Antioch Lithonia Missionary Baptist Church, which is under the leadership of Pastor James C. Ward. I thank you, Pastor, for the teachings I have received from you for the past sixteen years. I am honored to have you as my shepherd and spiritual father. Keep allowing God to give you the vision for the sheep you are held accountable for. I also thank Sister Idell Ward, the first lady of Antioch-Lithonia.

Thank you to my intercessory prayer partners, Sister Frances Anderson and Dr. Susan Jones. I love you, and I feel honored just to know you.

To my husband, John; my daughters, Brittany, Cortney, and

Akila; my granddaughters, Akira and Paris; and my grandson, Juelz, I thank God for all of you. Always strive to do what's right because your integrity is all you have.

To my mother, Margie; my sister, April; and my brother, Bruce Jr., always hold on to God's unchanging hand. He is the same yesterday, today, and forevermore.

In memory of my beloved grandmother Dora Hyman Woodard (September 20, 1909–February 28, 1997), may the Jacbaws you left behind have the desire to seek God the way we saw you seek Him throughout your entire life.

And finally in memory of my father, Elder Bruce Woodard (June 2, 1937–November 14, 2012), who has gone on to be with the Lord, I will see you again on the other side.

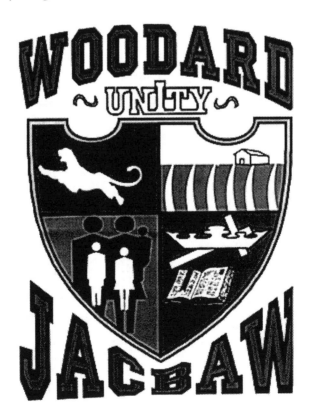

INTRODUCTION

A Visit to the Doctor

"WHY DO WE NEED SPIRITUAL checkups?" I'm glad you asked. We live in a world where it often appears that those who live non-Christian lives tend to prosper more than Christians do. As a result, Christians often try to mimic the actions of non-Christians to get by. In other words, we use non-Christian tactics to try to get ahead. We begin to give toxic things the freedom to come into our lives in order to help us cope with our daily problems. It's for this reason that it's extremely important to have a spiritual checkup on a regular basis.

Having a spiritual checkup hinders toxic things from forming in our bodies, and if they do form, we have access through Jesus Christ to destroy them. The Word of God says, "No weapon that is formed against thee shall prosper; and every tongue that shall rise against thee in judgment thou shalt condemn" (Isaiah 54:17).

Most of us make appointments with our regular doctors to make sure everything in our bodies is working in the manner that it should be, that our bodies are in good running order. When we neglect to do this, we discover that we have a severe problem that could have been avoided if we had scheduled an appointment to see a doctor.

Thus, we obtain the best diagnosis when we are open and honest with doctors. Think about it. When you are not honest with your doctor about your symptoms and problems, you have to make repeat visits. The doctor prescribes something for you based upon the symptoms and problems you have shared. When you do not get any better, you become frustrated because the doctor cannot seem to help you. All of this can be avoided if we are truly honest with our doctors at the onset of our symptoms and problems.

Likewise, on this Christian journey, we have to be honest and admit our weaknesses and problems to God so He can help us. If you know you have a problem with an area that will be discussed in this book, do not let pride get the best of you. Ask God for help.

Please use the sections specifically designated for answering the questions and journaling your thoughts located after each chapter to help you keep track of what the Holy Spirit shows you while reading this book. They have been strategically placed after each chapter to ensure that you focus on what has been discussed in that particular chapter before moving forward in your reading. I have purposely included my life experiences after the questions to ensure that my life experiences have no influence on your answers to the questions provided. In addition, I have included a Road Map and Prayer for Salvation at the end of this book to offer Christ to the unsaved. Upon accepting Jesus Christ as your personal savior, you will find a section designated to welcoming you to the family of God.

Let's see how well you do during your spiritual checkup.

Pray for God to speak to you before you turn this page!

CHAPTER 1

Checking Your Blood Pressure

How Much Pressure Can You Withstand as a Christian?

THE WORD OF GOD SAYS that we are peculiar people. Indeed, we are peculiar! As peculiar people our responses to unforeseen situations should make us stand out among others who may be experiencing similar circumstances. God is pleased with us when we do not allow difficult situations to shake our faith or affect our trust in Him. Consequently there should be something a little different about us that catches the non-Christian's eye when we are going through warring storms and trials.

Realistically you will face situations and circumstances on this Christian journey that you'll find extremely difficult to understand. But even through this, know that you are not alone and that God has not forsaken you. No, He is with you even during physical and mental despair. Remember that you are special to God. There is absolutely no obstacle that you will face that God in His infinite power cannot handle. God is larger than our problems, and that is praiseworthy. God deserves our praise because He called us out of darkness into His marvelous light.

> But ye are a chosen generation, a royal priesthood, an holy nation, a peculiar people; that ye should shew forth the praises of him who hath called you out of darkness into his marvelous light. (1 Peter 2:9)

God wants us to take solace in Him. He is the only one who can truly give us the relief we seek. He offers us consolation that can be found in no other place. As a Christian you are able to freely give the pressure that you are under to Jesus and therefore have rest. The Word of God says, "Come unto me, all ye that labour and are heavy laden, and I will give you rest" (Matthew 11:28).

We should not allow ourselves to get to the point of being so overwhelmed that we forget that Jesus is our burden-bearer. Because you are God's child, you may give your problems to Him when they present themselves. Do not allow yourself to react like non-Christians do when you are faced with problems. The world reacts to obstacles in one way, but we should react to them in the Christian way.

If our reactions to a situation is not handled delicately through a spiritual checkup, the problem, which may seem minor in the very beginning, will soon turn into something major.

When we visit the doctor, most of our physical problems cannot be seen with the naked eye. As a result, the doctor takes advantage of technology and runs tests to discover and diagnose the problem, which aids in offering solutions. Likewise, as Christians we need to allow the Holy Spirit to aid us at the onset of our problems.

The Holy Spirit's job is to lead and direct us to all truth. The Holy Spirit will let you know not only the cause but the location of the problem. The Holy Spirit will further instruct you on how to recover from the problem. In order to have a speedy recovery, you must listen intently to what the Holy Spirit is instructing you to do. Follow the precise instructions that you are given through prayer and intuition. Otherwise you will feel as if you have just put a Band-Aid on to cover up the problem you are attempting to cope with, and it may possibly return.

There may be times when you feel like you just cannot take it anymore, or you may simply feel like just giving up. This is when you need to thank God for the Holy Spirit. Take advantage of the Comforter who came to us when Jesus left. When you feel like you want to give up, make an appointment with the Holy Spirit and set aside time to read the Word of God. The Holy Spirit will lead you to the truth of God's Word.

When you accepted Jesus Christ as your personal Lord and Savior, that alone gave you an open door to everything you need. The Word of God says Jesus came not only so that you might have life but so that you would have it more abundantly. Unlike our Adversary, who wants to destroy us, Jesus is on our side and wants us to live in peace. The Adversary wants to steal, kill and destroy your peace. "The thief cometh not, but for to steal, and to kill, and to destroy; I am come that they might have life, and that they might have it more abundantly" (John 10:10).

Regardless of the type of pressure you may be under at this present time, please know that your pressure is not greater than God. God is concerned about the pressure in your life. In fact, He is so concerned that He sent His only begotten Son, Jesus Christ, to overcome the world just for you! You have direct access to God through Jesus Christ. We can call on Him any time we need to. He never sleeps or slumbers, and His ears are always open to our concerns.

I want to ask you a question. Are you calling on your Father? You see, this is how to get relief from the pressure you're under. Remember, now that you are a child of God you don't have to go through anything alone anymore. The Word of God says that He will never leave you or forsake you.

I know you may be feeling pressured even right now in the very midst of reading this book. However, know that as a child of God, weeping may endure for a night but joy comes in the morning. I can't stress enough that we are being watched as children of God. The world is constantly looking for excuses not to change its way of living. Don't allow yourself to be that stumbling block, for someone else's salvation is at stake. You may be the only Bible that person ever sees.

As Christians we have to set the stage for non-Christians. The Bible teaches us to stand firm on the Word of God. Because we are the salt of the earth and possess the substance of God's Word, we should not allow ourselves to unfold when we are faced with pressure. We have to get in the habit of calling on our helper, who was left to us by Jesus Christ. Make it a habit to call on the Holy Spirit to help you withstand the pressure of the world. This is significant because our Christian lifestyles should be the salt that seasons the world to make it lively just as salt seasons our food to make it tasty.

> Ye are the salt of the earth: but if the salt has lost his savour, wherewith shall it be salted? It is thenceforth good for nothing, but to be cast out, and to be trodden under foot of men. (Matthew 5:13)

Getting your spiritual checkup is vital. Allow the Holy Spirit to examine you. Always be obedient when the Holy Spirit detects a problem and directs you to adjust an area of your life. Call on Jesus to help you with the adjustment when the pressure seems too intense for you to handle alone. He is your friend, and He is always ready to come to your rescue!

It's extremely dangerous to allow pressure to continue to build in your body. If you ignore the warning signs, you're headed for big trouble. If it goes on undetected, a minor pressure problem is likely to cause you to become perplexed. Moreover, you may begin to distrust God's Word, which consequently leads to a dead-end road and you will be conquered by your pressure.

Give thanks to God, for He loves us enough that He gave His only begotten Son, Jesus Christ, to die on the cross just for you and for me. Jesus is our help and our strength. He makes intercessions for us daily as He sits at the right hand of the Father. Give the pressure that you are under to Jesus by calling on Him for help. I assure you that He will help!

This concludes your first spiritual checkup.

Questions regarding your first spiritual checkup

1. What do you think God thinks about you as His Christian patient?

   _____

   _____

   _____

2. What did the Holy Spirit reveal to you during your examination?

   _____

   _____

   _____

3. Is your temperature gauge right now reading hot, cold, or lukewarm?

   _____

My Life Experience in This Area

I received a call from my daughter in the middle of the day. She telephoned to tell me that the water had just been cut off. I didn't have enough money to pay the bill and still had two days left before payday. My daughter had just given birth a few weeks earlier. We needed water to make formula for the baby and to bathe ourselves. I didn't panic. I didn't even worry. I called on the Lord, Jesus. I reminded Him of His Word. I said, "Lord, You said that You would be a very present help in times of trouble, and I need you to touch someone's heart and make a way for me."

I telephoned the water company and stated that my water had been cut off. I told them I had a two-week-old baby in the house and needed the water to be turned back on as soon as possible. I was told that it takes three days to turn the water back on once it has been shut off.

I telephoned back a second time to speak to a manager and was sent to someone's voicemail. I then decided to leave work an hour early to try to get there before the office closed. I still had hope because one of the customer service representatives I had spoken to earlier told me that for an extra $50.00, the water could be put back on if the payment was made by 2:00 p.m. Well, I knew that wouldn't do me any good because it was already 4:00 p.m. However, I arrived at the water company at about 4:20 p.m. I was planning on paying with a check because I knew that it would take at least two days for the check to clear my bank account, and by then the money would be available.

God showed favor as He always does when you trust Him. I went to the window to make the payment with a check and was told that I didn't have to pay the extra $50.00 and that if my water was not turned back on by that same night, it would be turned back on sometime the next day. In the very midst of my sharing this life experience with you and while I am still typing, the water was turned back on at 8:00 p.m. this same night. Hallelujah! Glory to Your name.

What has the Holy Spirit shown me about my blood pressure?

Journaling

_____

_____

_____

_____

_____

_____

_____

_____

_____

_____

_____

CHAPTER 2

Checking Your Temperature

How Much Steam Can You Handle before You Blow Off?

THE WORD OF GOD SAYS to grow angry but sin not. Although the previous chapter discusses the ramifications of ignoring minor pressure problems, which can often progress to anger, please know that as Christians we will ultimately become angry at times. The anger becomes a problem when we allow our anger to cause us to sin. It is vital that you listen very closely to the Holy Spirit, who tells you exactly what He is directed to tell you.

It's in our best interests as Christians to strive to control our temperatures, which regulates our anger. We don't want our uncontrollable steam to blow off and cause someone to stumble. When we allow this to happen, we no longer represent the light of Jesus Christ, but we symbolize darkness. We cannot represent the light of Jesus and darkness at the same time. Sin places us in a dark place. When we become angry and our anger causes us to sin, we need to quickly ask God and the person whom we've offended for forgiveness to ensure that we do not lie down at night with unforgiving hearts. "Be ye angry, and sin not: let not the sun go down upon your wrath" (Ephesians 4:26).

The Word of God says, "A fool's wrath is presently known, but a prudent man covereth shame" (Proverbs 12:16). Simply put, a fool shows his annoyance at once, but a wise man overlooks an insult. There will be times when you are faced with hurtful words. Sometimes those words may even seem to cut right through you. Despite the rhyme that many of us used to say as children, "Sticks and stones may break my bones, but words will never hurt me," words really do hurt. But as Christians we are expected to grow angry but sin not. We are not to conform to the way of the world because Jesus has already overcome the world. When you have taken on as much as you think you can possibly handle and feel like you are going to explode, yell out Jesus' name. He will come to your aid. He has already made a way of escape for any temptation that you should encounter.

However, we do have a cross to carry on this Christian journey. We will have trials and tribulations on this earth. This should not be shocking to you. As such, best results are achieved by being silent and listening to the Holy Spirit. Having a spiritually keen ear will allow you to hear the precise instructions to achieve victory when you are going through trials and tribulations. We have to train ourselves to be silent unless the Holy Spirit directs us to speak. This is significant because speaking out of the will of God often leads to our steam blowing off. Moreover, some of our greatest battles can be won simply by being silent. "Be still, and know that I am God: I will be exalted among the heathen, I will be exalted in the earth. The Lord of hosts is with us; the God of Jacob is our refuge" (Psalm 46:10–11).

How many times have you blown off and later regretted it? Were you thinking to yourself, *I wish I would have handled that situation a little differently? I should have just kept my mouth shut.* Let's be realistic. It's very hard to witness to people who have seen us blow off. That's why it's so hard to witness to our unsaved family members. They are going by what they've seen us do in the past.

As the Christian you have to be the bigger person in situations that may cause your steam to blow off. We are expected to control our temperature. As a matter of fact, we should be able to walk into a room that is full of strife, and our very presence should bring calmness. Stop letting the Devil have his way in this area of your life. You are peculiar, and peculiar people stand out amongst the crowd. The Devil knows what upsets us and will try us in that area. But thank God that He knows what upsets us as well. Call on God, and He will help you in that area. Resist the Devil, and he will flee from you.

Work on controlling your temperature. Don't allow your steam to build up because the pressure will eventually blow off. Ask God to give you peace so that you will remain calm. God loves you, and He is on your side. Days will come when you feel weakened, and on those days it may not take very much for your steam to blow off. Ask God for forgiveness and move on. Do not beat up on yourself when your steam blows off. Repent and keep it moving. This may be an area in your life where God has to really help you. The problem escalates when you don't ask for forgiveness, which makes moving on more difficult.

Try your best to let your light shine as much as possible so that God will be pleased with you. Stop trying to be people-pleasers because God is the most important person that we should strive to please. Allow God to monitor your thermostat to determine if you are too hot or too cold because we don't want to be so religious that we are no earthly good. More specifically we don't want our light to shine so brightly that it blinds those with whom we come into contact but shines enough to allow our light to direct others to Jesus. Listen closely to the Holy Spirit to see which way your light needs adjusting.

This concludes your second spiritual checkup.

Questions regarding your second spiritual checkup

1. When was the last time your steam caused you to blow off?

   _____

   _____

   _____

2. Did you repent after you blew off steam?

   _____

   _____

   _____

3. Did you go back and apologize to the person to whom you blew up on?

   _____

   _____

   _____

4. Did the person accept your apology? If not, was your apology really sincere? Explain how you apologized.

_____

_____

_____

My Life Experience in This Area

I was not having a really good day at work. It seemed like everyone I served that day had an attitude. You see, I was allowing my steam to grow. My customer service skills are normally pretty good, but it was just *one of those days*. As the day wore on, I served another customer at the counter who had a question that one of my coworkers needed to handle.

I explained the situation to that coworker and did not like the response that I was given. As stated, it had already been a very trying day, and I allowed my steam to blow. I immediately told the coworker, "How am I supposed to know that? I don't do the job that you do. All of you handle the same job in a different manner, and that's why we don't know what to tell anyone!"

Of course the coworker retaliated, and I just walked off. After I cooled off, I felt ashamed. I asked God to forgive me in Jesus' name, and the next day I went to the coworker and apologized for what I had said. I told the coworker that I should have kept my mouth shut and just not said anything. I also told the coworker that I had had a bad day the previous day. I apologized, and the coworker accepted my apology.

Now all of this could have been avoided if I had just been silent and called on the name of the Lord to help me. Had I called on Him in the very beginning when I could see it was not going to be a good day, the rest of my day would have been peaceful. But I neglected to call on Him for strength when I needed to. Thank God for the Holy Spirit convincing me that I could go back to my coworker and apologize. I'm sure it shocked my coworker for me to come back and apologize, but as a Christian I knew that it was the right thing for me to do. This doesn't mean that we aren't going to make mistakes, but when we do make mistakes, we should correct them when they are brought to our attention by way of the Holy Spirit. You see, the Devil certainly got no joy from that situation. To God be the glory.

What has the Holy Spirit shown me about my temperature?

Journaling

CHAPTER 3

Checking Your Ears

What Are You Allowing to Come into Your Mind through Your Ears?

THE WORD OF GOD SAYS faith cometh by hearing ... and hearing by the Word of God. What are you allowing to come into your mind by way of your ears to hinder your faith?

The opposite of faith is doubt. When you have doubt in your life, you are simply not trusting God. God is not pleased with us when we don't trust Him because without faith it is impossible to please Him. We are to exhibit "right now" faith in this present time because the faith we had on yesterday does us no good today since the cares of yesterday are gone. "Now faith is the substance of things hoped for, the evidence of things not seen" (Hebrews 11:1).

The best medicine to rid ourselves of doubt is hearing the Word of God. We all have been given a measure of faith. When we are going through the storms of life, we have to believe that no matter how alone we may feel, God has not forgotten and abandoned us. He will simply remove the storm, see us through the storm, or carry us through the storm. I heard a minister once say that storms serve two purposes. Either they come to make us stronger, or they come to bring glory to God. In saying this, as Christians we need to call on God at the onset of a storm. We often wait to call on God to help us as a last resort when everything else we have tried has failed. God should be *first* in our lives. He wants us to call on Him first. This is what pleases God. You have to trust God to make a way when you don't see a way.

During vacation Bible school in 2006 the teacher made a comment that intrigued me. He said that our tears were fine but that we had to move on past our tears because God was moved by our faith and not by our tears. That is such a powerful statement. God is indeed moved by our faith. He knows the circumstances that we are going through, and He wants us to trust Him in every one of our situations. As I was writing this chapter, the Holy Spirit gave me the following acronym for the word faith to help us remember to trust Him in every situation.

*F*ollowers
*A*lways
*I*n Every Situation
*T*rust
*H*im

Don't allow yourself to fail the faith test. The Bible teaches that with the faith of a mustard seed we can move mountains. The Word of God is true. As Christians we don't need carnal weapons because we have faith. It stands strongly and powerfully alone above the world's weapons. When you reach that point in your life when you feel like everything is targeted against you and it seems impossible for you to attain victory, sometimes it is because you have allowed that toxic thing called doubt to creep into your mind and take over your thoughts.

Once doubt enters your mind, the Devil has you on his playing field, where he begins to call the shots. I once heard a man of God say, "The Devil is good at his game, but you have to be on your game too." This is so true because the Devil loves trying to take over your mind. On the Devil's playing field, he likes to keep you busy thinking about negative things. This will not work in God's realm. To be on God's team, you must think on positive things. When something negative enters your mind, immediately think on something good. If you practice this enough, it will truly become a habit.

Stop giving the Enemy the home court advantage! Resist the Devil, and he will flee. You can do all things through Christ, who strengthens you. Let your ears hear positive words flowing from your mouth. There is already enough negativity in the world. Let godly words flow from your mouth. Let your words uplift and brighten someone's day. People should be able to see Jesus in you. Remember, as Christians our lifestyles may be the only Bible some people ever see. Because we are Christians, we are the devil's opponent, as such; we should submit our lifestyles to God while resisting the devil so that he will flee from us. "Submit yourselves therefore to God. Resist the devil, and he will flee from you" (James 4:7).

The Word of God says that we should guard our ears the way our mouth tastes food. If you're eating something and don't like the taste of it, you spit it out and throw the rest away. Well, likewise if you hear negative talk, leave the area. If it is not feasible to leave the area, take control of the conversation by changing the course of the communication. "For the ear trieth words, as the mouth tasteth meat" (Job 34:3).

If you are always around negative people, negativity will soon become a part of your life. Your talk will become negative because that is what you are allowing your ears to transmit to your mind. You will know when you have allowed yourself to be around negativity too long because the Holy Spirit will tell you. Listen very closely to the Holy Spirit. He tells you what He is directed to tell you. God sincerely wants you to pass the test, not fail.

As Christians we are to bring light to dark situations. If hanging around negative people was one of your weaknesses before you came to Christ, pray and ask God to lead you in what to say to bring light into the conversation. Don't allow yourself to get caught up in the hype of negative talking or thinking.

You have to continuously safeguard your ears. You are responsible for what you allow your ears to hear. There is no excuse for allowing negativity to be spoken into your life. If faith cometh by hearing and hearing by the Word of God, what brings about doubt? The only sensible answer has to be not hearing the Word of God. And if you're not hearing the Word of God, then you are hearing the Enemy's word. As Christians we already know that the Enemy's word is a lie because not only is he a liar but he is the father of lies. Again, God's Word is true.

The Enemy wants us to feed off of negativity. Birds of a feather flock together. Negativity begets negativity. What are your surroundings like? Who are you allowing yourself to entertain? Misery loves misery. In other words, if you are around negative people all of the time and are allowing yourself to hear negativity on a daily basis, you will eventually become negative because that's what your ears are hearing.

As Christians it hurts our credibility as witnesses when we are negative. How can we share the Good News of the Gospel and then turn right around and allow negative things to flow out of our mouths into someone's ears? Keep in mind that when we speak negative words to someone, our ears are listening too. Those negative words bounce right back on us. In fact, we may be the cause for a lot of the negative thinking that goes on in our own minds. Ask the Lord to renew your mind on a daily basis. You will be surprised by how fast those negative thoughts leave your mind when your mind is being renewed daily by Jesus Christ.

Just as faith and positive words go together, doubt and negative words go together. Faith is trusting God no matter how hard the situation may seem. Whenever your faith gets weak, think on other times when God has made a way out for you when you could see no way out for yourself. God is the same yesterday, today, and forevermore. It is for this reason that sharing testimonies play a significant role for others.

In order to have a testimony, you have to go through the test. Testimonies are both positive and uplifting. When you share your testimony with someone, your ears are also listening. This simply means that while you are sharing your testimony, you are encouraging yourself too.

To guard your ears, it's okay to walk away when negativity is being spoken. Your reputation should speak for itself. It should be understood among all those with whom you associate that if something negative is taking place, you will have no part of it. Your name should not be associated with negativity. If it is, from this day forward you should strive to change your reputation. Trust me! People will notice.

This concludes your third spiritual checkup.

Questions regarding your third spiritual checkup

1. Are you allowing negative words to come into your mind through your ears?

   _____

   _____

   _____

2. Is your faith easily hindered? If so, what do you think is causing your faith to be easily hindered?

   _____

   _____

   _____

3. What are you expecting to happen by having your mind renewed daily by Jesus?

   _____

   _____

   _____

My Life Experience in This Area

When you are a babe in Christ, it is so easy to think upon negative things. I, too, was a negative thinker. I realized how powerful positive thinking and speaking was and how it could change my life. I remember when I couldn't see past the moment or past the bill that was due. I was always trying to figure things out; my brain seemed to always be in a muddle. My mind was constantly thinking negative thoughts. "How am I going to pay this? How am I going to pay that?" I'd exclaim. Then I'd pray, "Oh, Lord, help me!" Then two seconds later I was thinking, *What in the world am I going to do?* That was the problem! I was too busy trying to figure it out myself instead of giving it to God. I couldn't see beyond even the first problem! I gave up on God without even realizing it!

Oh, life is so much more wonderful now! Remember, Jesus said that He came so that we might have life … and have life more abundantly. I still have situations that I deal with as far as bills go and the day-to-day trials and tribulations that we all have on this earth, but glory be to God that I don't have sleepless nights any longer. I pray about it and talk to God about it, and then I go to sleep. I remind God of His Word. My ears now hear me calling on the name of Jesus. My ears now hear me praising God, and my ears now hear me encouraging others because I encourage myself while I am encouraging them.

One of my favorite scriptures is Romans 8:28, "All things work together for the good of those that love God and are called according to his purpose." I don't care what type of situation I am going through. I remind God of His Word. He cannot lie. That means it has to work together for the good. I now speak positive words to my situations.

Another scripture that I like to keep in mind and speak when I'm going through trials and tribulations is Psalm 46:1, "Lord, you said that you would be a very present help in the time of trouble. I'm in trouble right now, and I need your help. You are a God that cannot lie, and I need you."

There are so many advantages to being a Christian that we choose to ignore. We have the Word of God and need to speak the Word of God boldly. Jesus even told the Devil, "It is written, Man shall not live by bread alone, but by every word that proceedeth out of the mouth of God" (Matthew 4:4). We have no reason to worry. Jesus has already overcome the world. "In the world ye shall have tribulation: but be of good cheer; I have overcome the world" (John 16:33). As God moves in your life by answering you when you call on Him, you will see your faith begin to grow just as the mustard seed grows. Father God, we thank You for Your Word, which increases our faith.

What has the Holy Spirit shown me about my ears?

Journaling

_____

_____

_____

_____

_____

_____

_____

_____

_____

_____

_____

CHAPTER 4

Checking Your Mouth

What Are You Letting Flow from Your Mouth by Way of the Tongue?

THE WORD OF GOD SAYS to keep thy tongue from evil and thy lips from speaking deceit. Our mouths were created to praise God. When we use our mouths to speak evil, we are doing exactly what the Enemy wants us to do. This brings no glory to God and damages our reputations. "Keep thy tongue from evil and thy lips from speaking guile" (Psalm 34:13).

We hold the power of life and death in our tongues. Who are you killing with your tongue? Who have you committed premeditated murder against by channeling thoughts toward revenge? In other words, how often have you thought about and preplanned what you were going to say to someone far in advance of reaching him or her? Perhaps you thought this: *I am going to tell such and such a piece of my mind when I see him or her!*

The tongue is an indisputably dangerous weapon when we use it to demean people instead of using it to encourage and glorify God. It's imperative that we strive to make strenuous efforts to tame our tongues because once hurtful, bitter words have flowed from our mouths, the intent to convey pain has successfully been attained. It is impossible for us to retrieve words once they have been released from our mouths.

Perhaps you are holding a grudge against someone right now for something that he or she may have said to you on a prior occasion. Although the exact words may have escaped your mind, the hurt that followed the words still lingers. This is a prime example of how dangerous the tongue can be when it's not used for exhortation. "Death and life are in the power of the tongue: and they that love it shall eat the fruit thereof" (Proverbs 18:21).

How many times have you used your tongue to cut someone down? Do you find yourself having to go back to apologize to people whom you've offended? It's easy for us to remember when someone has said something hurtful to us, but do we remember the hurtful words that we may have released to someone else? Guess what? I bet they remember our hurtful words.

The tongue is an amazingly powerful weapon. We speak to people and move mountains through our mouths by way of the tongue, and in a mere ten seconds we can use that same tongue to degrade someone. We shouldn't praise God with our mouths and then turn right around and use them to tear someone down. This allows our Adversary to use us. Remember that the Devil is conniving. Most of the time we don't even realize the Devil is actually using us. That's why it's so important for us to get our spiritual checkups on a regular basis. We have to stay in the Word of God to allow the Holy Spirit to show us whether we are hot, cold, or lukewarm while we are on this spiritual journey.

The tongue should be used to uplift people, not tear them down. It is imperative that we cease talking about people behind their backs and then turning right around and smiling to their faces. God is not pleased with us when we allow the Devil to use us in this area. We have to stop justifying our actions in talking to and treating people in the manner that we do. There is nothing for us to justify. We need to leave that job to the Holy Spirit. The Holy Spirit will let us know whether our actions are in line with the Word of God or not.

In addition, the Holy Spirit will let us know if we have said something untruthful. In God's eyes there is no such thing as a *little white lie*. There is no *gray area*. Either we are telling the truth, or we're telling a lie. A sin is a sin. I don't care if you consider it to be a little sin or a big sin. Don't let the Devil convince you that it's no big deal because it was just a little lie. The Devil does not want you to succeed on this Christian journey. The Devil tries to destroy the knowledge that you have of God and wants you to think that God won't hold you accountable for small lies. Remember, a sin is when we know that we should do right and still choose to do wrong. The Holy Spirit will convict us when we are wrong. Now we may choose to ignore the Holy Spirit, but our choosing to ignore the Holy Spirit does not make our sins disappear.

Always strive to do what is right because your integrity is all you have. As Christians we should walk in the utmost integrity. Regardless of who is watching us, our number-one thought should be that God is watching us. If His eye is on the sparrow, we know He's watching us too. He's watching to see how we're going to handle this trial or how we're going to handle this test. He's watching to see what's going to flow out of our mouths if things don't go our way during the trial.

Because we will have trials and tribulations on this earth, we need to use our tongue to praise God while we are going through difficult times. This not only pleases God but confuses the Enemy. Strive to praise God with all that you have. It's not always going to be easy to praise God when you're going through trials and tribulations, but once you start praising and thanking Him, you will receive peace in your situation.

Use your mouth by way of your tongue to receive your blessings through praise. When praises go up, blessings surely come down. Continue to do what is right in the eyes of God. Don't grow weary. Your season is on the way. You may not understand why you are going through what you are going through, but God knows. There's definitely a blessing on the other side if you don't grow weary and give up. "And let us not be weary in well doing: for in due season we shall reap, if we faint not" (Galatians 6:9).

We have to be extremely careful not to forfeit our blessings by fainting and growing weary. Sometimes our blessings show up through peace, joy, sound mind, or even an answered prayer for a relative or friend. It's easy for us to miss our blessing if we are looking in the wrong direction. You may be expecting a blessing to come in a certain fashion, and God may send the blessing in a whole different arena. God is just that awesome. We never really know what to expect of Him or how He is going to show up. We just know that He shows up. Even when it seems all is impossible, praise Him anyway. Use your tongue to praise God. He is so worthy of our praise. Moreover, praise is powerful and helps us obtain the victory.

Focus on the goodness of the Lord and ask the Holy Spirit to help you. After all, that's why Jesus said He would send the Comforter to us. You have to use what you have with you to receive what you want. We need to keep praise in our mouths because God inhabits the praises of His people. Thank You, Father God, for living in our praises.

This concludes your fourth spiritual checkup.

Questions regarding your fourth spiritual checkup

1. Have you allowed the Devil to use you to speak evil or deceit?
    If so, did you correct the situation?

    _____

    _____

    _____

2. Are you guilty of telling *little white lies*? If yes, did the Holy Spirit
    convict you? Explain.

    _____

    _____

    _____

    _____

    _____

    _____

3. Have you been using your tongue to praise the Lord or for
    something else?

    _____

    _____

    _____

4. What type of reputation do you think you have? Would God be pleased with your reputation?

_____

_____

_____

_____

_____

5. At this point, is your temperature hot, cold, or lukewarm? Explain.

_____

_____

_____

_____

My Life Experience in This Area

Once I was in a situation in which someone was saying things to me that I didn't take too kindly to. Although my flesh wanted to take over and snap right back at the person, the Holy Spirit helped me hold my peace and keep my thoughts to myself. In other words, the Holy Spirit helped me not use my tongue to do damage. You see, you have to know when to call on the Comforter's help. You don't ask for His help after you have reacted to the situation. You call on Him before you react.

On this particular occasion I used my mouth to speak positive things. I told the Devil that I knew this was a test and that I was going to pass this test. I told the Devil that he was just wasting his time because no matter what he did the situation was going to work together for the greatest good because everything I had experienced was going to collaborate with each other to ensure my victory. Immediately after I spoke those words to the Devil, the person came to me and apologized.

Do you see how that same situation could have come out totally different had I used my mouth to speak what my flesh wanted me to say? God still wants a pure heart. Although I didn't react back with my mouth by way of the tongue, I still thought about saying something back. I asked God to forgive me for my thoughts. The Devil got no joy out of this situation, and God was glorified. We praise Your holy name.

What has the Holy Spirit shown me about my mouth?

Journaling

_____

_____

_____

_____

_____

_____

_____

_____

_____

_____

_____

CHAPTER 5

Checking Your Eyes

What Are You Allowing Your Eyes to Catch Vision of Daily?

THE WORD OF GOD SAYS to write the vision and make it plain. What vision are your eyes constantly focusing on? Are you focusing on earthly things or eternal things?

Are you seeking first the kingdom of God and His righteousness so that all other things can be added? As Christians our focus should be on all things eternal. Keep your eyes focused on the prize because you will receive your reward in heaven. "But seek ye first the kingdom of God, and his righteousness; and all these things shall be added unto you" (Matthew 6:33).

When Peter was walking on water toward Jesus, he began to sink after he took his focus off of Jesus. Just like Peter, when we begin to take our focus off of Jesus, we cause ourselves to sink in our circumstances too. As our focus remains on Jesus, we are able to do some amazingly remarkable things through the Holy Spirit. This is possible because the Word of God says, "Greater is He that is in you, than he that is in the world" (1 John 4:4b).

What are your spiritual desires from God? Are you allowing God to use you on a regular basis? If so, you already know that this requires spiritual discipline. We have to stay focused on God to be effective. You see, our eyes are very important components of our bodies. Our eyes can be a hindrance to us if we don't allow them to stay focused on God.

> The light of the body is the eye: if therefore thine eye be single, thy whole body shall be full of light. But if thine eye be evil, thy whole body shall be full of darkness. If therefore the light that is in thee be darkness, how great is that darkness! (Matthew 6:22–23)

If God shows you a vision, don't lose focus of the vision that He has given you. He will bring it to pass. Don't faint even if the vision does not manifest in your time frame. He will not bring it to pass until He knows you're ready for it. It's just like the writing of this book. When the Holy Spirit led me to write this book in 2008, I had no idea at that time that it would not get published until 2013. Suppose I had given up on God's promise to me. God prepares us for everything He shows us so that we will not be caught off guard. He will give you the provision for every vision that He gives you. Be cautious about sharing the vision God has given you. It's your vision, not someone else's. Other people may not understand the vision because it's not theirs. What God has for you is for you, not for the person with whom you may be sharing the vision.

Likewise, if God gives someone else a vision and he or she shares it with you, be careful that you don't put that vision down either because God is awesome. He has a purpose for us all. You need to stay focused on what God has for you. Allow God to use you. Keep in mind that

He may use you to help someone else's vision come to pass. God does not have to work through us, but He *chooses* to so that we can give Him glory. Are you taking credit for the work God does through you? If so, from this day forward be careful not to take credit for God's work. Keep your eyes focused on God, and this will not happen.

The Bible says that without a vision the people will perish. Take hold of the visions and dreams that God gives you. A vision from God is a promise, and He cannot go back on His Word. He will bring it to pass. The promises of God are still yea and amen. Don't allow anyone to turn you around or get you off of the path that God has you on. You're on that path for a reason. God comes from any direction He chooses.

There will be stop signs and yield signs on your path, but if God leads you down the path, you will get to your final destination. I don't care how many curves you encounter on your path. Just hold on and stay in your lane. Trust God to manifest the vision He has shown you. You cannot go wrong if you allow your eyes to stay focused on the vision that God has for you. You are special. God loves you, and God will use you to do His will. "For all the promises of God in him are yea, and in him Amen unto the glory of God by us" (2 Corinthians 1:20).

The promises of God are not manifested to the naked eye. You have to remember that spiritual things cannot be seen in the carnal world. When your eyes have been spiritually opened, you no longer see things the way a worldly person sees them. Stop looking at your circumstances and situations with the naked eye. Stay focused on God. Everything happens for a reason, and even if you don't believe that, you know the Bible states that all things work together for the good for those who love God and are called according to His purpose. In other words, if something happens to you that you don't think should happen to you, don't worry about it. It will work together for the good anyhow. "And we know that all things work together for good to them that love God, to them who are the called according to his purpose" (Romans 8:28).

Stand firm on the Word of God at all times. Do not waiver in His Word. We are often strong in the Word on Sunday, but as soon as Monday morning rolls around we're right back into our negative moods. Our eyes should be the sight for someone who is still blind in the world. How can we lead if the Holy Spirit is not leading us? The Bible states that we cannot correct someone who has a speck in his or her eye if we have a beam in our own eye. "Thou hypocrite, first cast out the beam out of thine own eye: and then shalt thou see clearly to cast out the mote out of thy brother's eye" (Matthew 7:5).

Your eyes need to stay focused on the Word of God. Read the Word of God and then read the Word of God again. The Bible says, "Study to shew thyself approved unto God, a workman that needeth not be ashamed, rightly dividing the word of truth" (2 Timothy 2:15). The Word of God has to get down into our hearts. The Word of God says, "Seek, and ye shall find; knock, and it shall be opened unto you" (Matthew 7:7). Use your eyes to seek the scriptures. The answer to every situation that we may possibly go through is in the Word of God.

God does not want you to perish from a lack of knowledge. He wants you to be fruitful. He wants you to live a fruitful life. Take hold of the visions that God shows you and seek after spiritual things, and you shall find them. Trust Him, and He shall bring them to pass in your life.

This concludes your fifth spiritual checkup.

Questions regarding your fifth spiritual checkup

1. Are you focusing on earthly things or eternal things? Explain.

   _____

   _____

   _____

2. Has God shown you a vision that has come to pass? Explain.

   _____

   _____

   _____

   _____

   _____

   _____

3. Has God shown you a vision, and are you still awaiting it to come to pass? Explain.

   _____

   _____

   _____

4. Have you lost focus of the vision that God has shown you? Explain.

   _____

   _____

   _____

   _____

   _____

5. At this point, is your temperature hot, cold, or lukewarm? Explain.

_____

_____

_____

_____

My Life Experience in This Area

About six or seven months after the Holy Spirit revealed my gifts to me, I had a vision. I was contemplating going back to school to become a teacher. I had already started looking at courses to take and talking to people I knew who were already teaching. I remember I was sitting on the floor in my bedroom, not concentrating on anything in particular, and I saw a vision of about five or six windows. The only things that could be seen out of the windows were trees. I immediately knew that the vision represented real estate. I had no desire to become a realtor. It was the furthest thing from my mind. I'm sure God was testing me to see if I would pursue the vision. Remember, I said earlier in the chapter that when God gives you a vision, He will also give you the provision to make it happen. Well, I had been a member of my church for about eight years at the time. One of the deacons came up to me and asked me if I was a realtor. I told him no, and he said, "I sure thought you were a realtor." He added, "You know, it's easy to become a realtor. They have it now where you can do it online or either take classes at night." You see, the deacon had no idea of the vision God had just given me three days earlier. This discussion took place on a Saturday.

The very next day someone else came up to me in church and

asked me the very same thing. I told the person that I was not a realtor. I returned to work on Monday, and a customer came to my counter and showed me his realtor card. He had just gotten his license. At this time I said, "Okay, Lord. I understand." I immediately registered to take classes to become a licensed realtor. You see, not only did God give me the vision, but He also gave me the provision to make it happen. That is what God had for me at the moment. There is a time and place for everything under the sun. God is now using me to write this book.

I remember that people were asking me, "How did you know God meant real estate?" and I told them that I just knew. God has a way of letting you know what you are supposed to be doing. You just feel that it is right. You will have peace with your decision. I can honestly say that I think I talk to God more than I talk to anyone. When you have a personal relationship with Him, you know His voice, and He will surely direct your path.

Don't let anyone deter you from what God has for you. God may have allowed me to get my real estate license to help only one person or to include this life experience in this book. Whatever the case, He is so worthy because He gave me the vision and He has brought it to pass. God, You are so worthy.

What Has the Holy Spirit shown me about my eyes?

Journaling

_____

_____

_____

_____

_____

_____

_____

_____

_____

_____

_____

_____

CHAPTER 6

Checking Your Heart

What Are the True Intentions of Your Heart when Doing for Others?

THE WORD OF GOD SAYS that we are to love our neighbors as ourselves. The Word of God also says that what is done in secret will be rewarded openly. Let's be honest. What are the true intentions of your heart when you are doing things for others? Is it just for show or recognition? We have to really be careful in this area because it's so easy to become pleasers of men rather than God in this area. "Take heed that ye do not your alms before men, to be seen of them: otherwise ye have no reward of your Father which is in heaven" (Matthew 6:1).

If you did something good for someone and you had to share it with others, most likely you were trying to please man rather than God. If this was the case, you have already gotten your reward for that good deed that was done. However, there is nothing wrong with sharing if it's used for the purpose to bring glory to God through testimonies. Have you ever done a good deed for someone but then talked about the person behind his or her back after you did the good deed? God is not pleased with us when we do this. God used you to meet someone's need, and then you turned right around and allowed the Devil to step in and cause you to fail your test. Yes, I said your *test*. Although the other person is the one getting blessed through you by God, you are being tested by the true intentions of your heart for doing the deed in the first place. God knows the intentions of our heart.

> For the word of God is quick, and powerful, and sharper than any two-edged sword, piercing even to the dividing asunder of soul and spirit, and of the joints and marrow, and is a discerner of the thoughts and intents of the heart. (Hebrews 4:12)

If this is a problem that you know you have, repent and ask God to help you in this area. I promise you He will help you. We are blessed so that we can be a blessing to someone else! Think about it. Have you ever helped someone out financially or any other way and truly got joy from the act? You received joy because the true intentions of your heart were pure. God is just that amazing! I know it doesn't make sense in that you give up something yet you receive joy, but that's the way spiritual things work. They don't make sense in the natural because they are supernatural. "A merry heart maketh a cheerful countenance: but by sorrow of the heart the spirit is broken" (Proverbs 15:13).

Treat others the way you would like to be treated. You may be on the top right now, but you may fall to the bottom one day and need someone to help you. Allow God to continue to use you to bless others. You don't know whose answer to a prayer you may be. Besides, that same person that God is allowing you to bless right now may be the same person God allows to bless you in the future.

We should desire to have the heart of Christ. That's what set David apart from the rest. He was a man after God's own heart. This doesn't mean that he did no wrong. Not only was he an adulterous man, but he was also a murderer. But still God said that he was a man after His very own heart. "I have found David the son of Jesse, a man after mine own heart, which shall fulfil all my will" (Acts 13:22).

Just as the heart is needed for survival in the natural world, the heart is vital on our spiritual journey because what enters our heart will make or break us as Christians. For the Word of God says, "Keep thy heart with all diligence; for out of it are the issues of life" (Proverbs 4:23). You have to guard your heart. Are you a jealous-minded person? Do you somewhat feel joy when you know someone who has hurt you is going through a difficult period in his or her life? If so, this is the total opposite of what being a Christian is all about. It's okay if some of these issues hit home because that's the purpose of this book. You're just getting your spiritual checkup.

It's easy to fool people, but thankfully God cannot be fooled. He sees our hearts and only He knows the true intentions of our hearts. I'm sure there has probably been a time when you did something for someone that came straight from your heart and that person took it the wrong way and may have even gotten upset with you. If this is the case, don't be troubled because God knew the true intention of your heart. Remember that man judges you from the outside but God judges you from within. Always keep your intentions pure so that God will be pleased with you.

This concludes your sixth spiritual checkup.

Questions regarding your sixth spiritual checkup

1. Has someone blessed you in the past, and could you tell that it didn't truly come from his or her heart? Explain.

   _____

   _____

   _____

   _____

   _____

2. Have you ever blessed someone with something and talked about the person behind his or her back afterward? Explain.

   _____

   _____

   _____

   _____

3. Did the Holy Spirit convict you? If so, how did you handle the conviction?

   _____

   _____

   _____

   _____

4. Have you ever felt joy after you were a blessing to someone? Explain.

   _____

   _____

   _____

   _____

My Life Experience in This Area

Years ago when I was still a babe in Christ, I blessed someone financially. The intentions came truly from my heart. As a matter of fact, the person had no idea that I was about to bless him. I simply called the person on the phone to offer my help, and he accepted. You see, the problem at the time wasn't the true intentions of my heart because it started out pure. The problem came when I didn't like what the person was going to do with the blessing. Not only was I trying to be a blessing, but I was also trying to play God because the person wasn't going to use the blessing for what I had thought it needed to be used for. Boy, was I upset! It was my money, and I wanted it to be used the way I thought it should be used. I was really foolish back then! Even though I was a babe in Christ, I knew God was not pleased with me. I remember the incident as though it was yesterday. I went into my bathroom and got on my knees and talked to God about it. I told Him that I was mad because I didn't give the blessing to the person so that he could use it this way. I wanted him to use it another way. I was furious. Even though it was not done so that God could bless me, I told Him that I knew I was not going to be blessed because I had really regretted giving the person the blessing. I actually even told God that I could have used the blessing for myself. You see, I had made a sacrifice that was done in vain. God used me to answer someone's prayer, and I'm sure I failed my test.

During my prayer I asked God to change my heart and to forgive me for the way I was feeling. I thank God that I had enough knowledge of Him to go to Him for myself and repent. I can say that I truly learned my lesson during that test.

We don't determine how and why God is using us. Just be a willing vessel and make yourself available to Him. There have been numerous times when God has placed me in someone's heart and he or she has blessed me financially. God, I thank You for caring enough about us to place us in people's hearts so that You can bless us through them and receive the glory.

What has the Holy Spirit shown me about my heart?

Journaling

_____

_____

_____

_____

_____

_____

_____

_____

_____

_____

_____

_____

CHAPTER 7

Checking Your Breathing

What Toxic Things Are You Allowing to Enter Your Body?

THE WORD OF GOD SAYS to present your body as a living sacrifice. Are you presenting your body as a living sacrifice?

The sacrifices in the Book of Leviticus were said to be a "sweet smell" to God. What smell do you think God considers our sacrifices to be? "And he shall put the incense upon the fire before the Lord, that the cloud of the incense may cover the mercy seat that is upon the testimony, that he die not" (Leviticus 16:13).

We have to be serious about presenting our bodies as living sacrifices, which is our reasonable service. The Word of God says, "I beseech you therefore, brethren, by the mercies of God, that ye present your bodies a living sacrifice, holy, acceptable unto God, which is your reasonable service" (Romans 12:1). Our sacrifices are special and pleasing to God. Do you have the smell of Jesus, or do you have the smell of the world?

God loves the fragrance of Jesus Christ. Our bodies are the temple of God. If Jesus Christ is in us, then we are expected to smell like Him. "Now thanks be unto God, which always causes us to triumph in Christ, and maketh manifest the savour of his knowledge by us in every place" (2 Corinthians 2:14).

Because we are Christians, our lifestyles should not resemble the world's lifestyle. If it feels right or looks good, it still may not be okay for us. We should not lower our standards just to fit in with the crowd. We are peculiar people, and if we are allowing our bodies to be used and treated as the world does, we are not set apart. Stop trying to smell like the world. We should have the scent of Jesus Christ.

The sweet savour of Jesus covers the smell of our sins. In Christ we are a pleasure to God and a sweet aroma unto Him because Christ covers us with His righteousness. We carry the smell of Christ. Does your fragrance linger in the room long after you have departed? If not, what scent or odor is clouding the room long after you have left?

Remember that this is your spiritual checkup! You surely would not have a problem with a doctor suggesting that you need to start or stop doing certain things to better your health. Well, likewise this book will help you with your preventative maintenance in your spiritual walk with Christ. Allow this book to help you in areas in which you know you need improvement.

Having the scent of Jesus on you is important. When you have the scent of Jesus, His scent enters the room as you enter the room. You don't have to go directly into the kitchen to smell what is being cooked. Likewise people should smell the scent of Jesus on you from afar too. What smell are you leaving in the atmosphere when you depart from a room? You are of this world but not a part of this world. "I have given them thy word; and the world hath hated them, because they are not of the world, even as I am not of the world" (John 17:14).

Don't try to smell like the world by acting like secular people. If you go into a burning house, you smell the stench of smoke. If you go into a perfume shop, you come out smelling like perfume. Likewise if you allow yourself to do as the world does, which is against God's will, you, too, will smell like the world.

> Love not the world, neither the things that are in the world. If any man love the world, the love of the Father is not in him. For all that is in the world, the lust of the flesh, and the lust of the eyes, and the pride of life, is not of the Father, but is of the world. (1 John 2:15–16)

It is truly a sacrifice when we choose not to dress like the world, which often satisfies the lust of the flesh, lust of the eyes, and the pride of life and leads to our smelling like the world. We should keep covered up what needs to be covered up. This does not mean that we're not expected to dress nicely, but we need to keep in mind that we represent Christ.

Consider how children put on anything when we allow them to dress themselves. They are not concerned with whether their dress directly or indirectly impacts anyone other than themselves. They are apt to put on striped pants with flowered shirts along with fur boots on the hottest days of the summer. As mature adults we know this is absurd. "When I was a child I spake as a child, I understood as a child, I thought as a child. But, when I became a man, I put away childish things" (1 Corinthians 13:11).

Instead of dressing for the world, we need to dress up in the power of the Lord by putting on the whole armor that pleases God. Thus, be cautious about becoming too friendly with the world and worldly things. This causes great danger to our walk with Christ. Don't allow anyone or anything to take you out of the arms of Jesus because that's your safety zone. Taking on the smell of the world will often cause you to miss the will of God for your life. Don't allow the Devil to entice you with what he considers the sweet smell of this world because smells can be deceiving. Allow the sweet smell of Jesus Christ, your Savior, to be with you always.

This concludes your seventh spiritual checkup.

Questions regarding your seventh spiritual checkup

1. Are you presenting your body as a living sacrifice? If so, how?

_____

_____

_____

_____

_____

2. Does your smell resemble Jesus Christ or the world? Explain.

_____

_____

_____

3. Are you sometimes too friendly with the world? Explain.

_____

_____

_____

4. If Jesus came face-to-face with you right now, are there some things you would be ashamed of?

_____

_____

_____

5. What do you need to work the hardest on right now in your spiritual walk?

_____

_____

_____

My Life Experience in This Area

Because of the loss of my first spouse at the age of twenty-six, I was a single parent for most of my older two children's lives. They couldn't understand why I wouldn't allow them to wear what some of their peers were wearing. At the time I'm sure they thought I was the meanest mom around. I remember one time my middle daughter made the comment to one of her friends, "My mom don't play."

I didn't allow them to wear clothing that was too revealing. As they tried on clothes, they would ask me, "Is this too short?" They may have felt like outcasts, but I didn't care about what their peers thought about them. It was a matter of what was considered respectable dress in my eyes, not theirs.

God charged me to raise them in the correct way, and I knew I was going to be held accountable for how I raised them. I was trying to teach them at an early age the dangers associated with following certain crowds. I used to tell them, "Just because they sell it doesn't mean you have to buy it." I used to say to them all of the time, "If all of your friends go jump off of a cliff right now, would you go jump behind them?"

As they got old enough to shop for themselves, I would sometimes allow them to purchase what they wanted themselves. They didn't know I was really testing them. I'm not saying it was easy because there were many times I had to cut up clothing that was too revealing.

Moreover, we have to set the stage for our children and grandchildren. We have to teach them to not only be respectable but to also dress respectably. It is not unusual for our children to do as we do instead of as we say. If we allow our dress to blend in with the world, their dress will too.

What has the Holy Spirit shown me about my breathing?

Journaling

_____

_____

_____

_____

_____

_____

_____

_____

_____

_____

_____

CHAPTER 8

Best Diagnosis Comes from Sharing Symptoms/Problems with Your Doctor

Are You Honest with Jesus about Your Weaknesses?

THE WORD OF GOD SAYS that God knew you before you were formed in your mother's womb. He already knows everything there is to know about you, including your weaknesses. Although God is omniscience, He still wants you to share your concerns and weaknesses with Him freely. When Jesus died on the cross for you, He took on everything you could ever possibly face on this earth. Jesus has already overcome the world, and likewise you are more than a conqueror.

Jesus wants to be your best friend. He wants you to share your innermost thoughts with Him and trust Him with everything you have, including your weaknesses. Weaknesses are simply weights that wear us down. The Bible tells us to lay aside every weight and sin that so easily besets us. "Let us lay aside every weight, and the sin which doth so easily beset us, and let us run with patience the race that is set before us" (Hebrews 12:1). Jesus is there to pick up the weight when we lay it down. He wants to be your first choice and not your last resort. This is not possible when we are not honest with God about our weaknesses. The only way we can be cleansed of our sins is to confess them and ask for forgiveness through Jesus' name. Likewise you have to ask God for help with your weaknesses to be set free. Jesus is willing to help you because He took on our infirmities. "That it might be fulfilled which was spoken by Esaias the prophet, saying, Himself took our infirmities, and bare our sicknesses" (Matthew 8:17).

The answer to everything (and I do mean everything) comes from our heavenly Father above. Ask Him for help. Don't let pride get the best of you. That powerful word *pride* is an extremely dangerous one. Having pride can hinder your walk and set you up for a great fall on this Christian journey. God already knows what you need and what you're going through. He's just waiting for you to admit your weaknesses and call on Him to help you.

Jesus is your burden-bearer, your heavy-load carrier, your mind-regulator, and anything else you need Him to be. God said, "I am that I am. The Holy Spirit was sent to help you. Remember the Trinity; the three are one." Whatever you need for God to be, He said, "I am." There are no weaknesses or problems that you will encounter on this journey that God is not able to handle and see you through. Just be honest with God about them. He has the answer to them all. He is completely capable of not only meeting you right where you are but endowing you with the strength you need during weak moments. "My grace is sufficient for thee: for my strength is made perfect in weakness" (2 Corinthians 12:9).

In addition, the Word of God says to take pleasure in infirmities and distresses for Christ's sake, for when you are weak, then you are made strong. "Therefore I take pleasure in infirmities, in reproaches, in necessities, in persecutions, in distresses for Christ's sake: for when I am weak, then am I strong" (2 Corinthians 12:10).

Do you realize how blessed you are to have the Father, the Son, and the Holy Spirit in your life? The Trinity is working for you at all times! In other words, if you were in a hospital, you would have the creator and holder of the medicine, the doctor to prescribe it, and then the assistant to make sure you are taking the medicine correctly. Thus, while you are going through difficulties, be honest with God about what you are feeling. The key word is *through*. There is indeed a blessing on the other side of *through* because God will come to your aid and you shall have unspeakable joy. "Weeping may endure for a night, but Joy cometh in the morning" (Psalm 30:5b).

You will have trials and tribulations on this earth. But remember that Jesus is either walking beside you or carrying you through. Don't give up and don't give in! Joy will come in the morning. Remember that the darkest hour is just before dawn. Don't allow the Devil to convince you to give up before dawn arrives in your life. I encourage you to hold on because trouble will not last always. A change is on the way.

When we go to our regular doctor, we receive the best diagnosis when we are honest with him or her. The doctor prescribes something for you based on the symptoms and problems you have shared with him or her, and you may not get any better unless you are honest. Likewise on this Christian journey you have to be honest and admit all of your weaknesses to God so He can help you. If you know you have a problem in some of the areas that were mentioned in this book, don't let pride get the best of you. Ask God for help. You are expected to walk the straight and narrow. Anyone can walk on a wide road. As you pray, ask Jesus to help you.

Don't allow your Christian lifestyle to be a deterrent for someone who has not accepted Jesus Christ as his or her personal Savior. It is God's will that all men be saved. But God, being the good God that He is, has given us *all* free will. He will not force Himself upon us. We have to know the Word of God. We have to live the Word of God, and most importantly we have to trust the Word of God.

We are all given new mercies each morning. God gives us other opportunities to get it right, other opportunities to start anew. Don't allow the Enemy's word to deceive and discourage you on this Christian journey because if you don't faint, you will discover that everything you have sacrificed on this Christian journey has not been sacrificed in vain.

It is my desire that this book help you on your journey. You may not dot every "I" or cross every "T," but you are striving to be more like Jesus each day. There will be days when you feel you don't measure up. Shake it off and keep on moving.

Just as it is important to have a regular checkup from your doctor, it is as significant to have a spiritual checkup to allow the Holy Spirit to regulate your thermometer gauge. Being too hot, too cold, or lukewarm are all dangerous warning signs that require immediate attention. By making an appointment with the Holy Spirit, you will ensure that your temperature remains at a level that allows Jesus' light to shine through you. Continue to be blessed on this Christian journey as you finish the race you began when you accepted Jesus Christ as your personal Savior. Remember that God loves you, and His love covers a multitude of things, including your sins and mistakes. Don't get discouraged in this race because if you don't faint, you will eventually reach the finish line.

The goal is for you to reach the finish line while your lifestyle points others toward the finish line, where we will spend eternity in heaven with our heavenly Father and Jesus Christ. Aren't you looking forward to singing in that heavenly choir where we will ultimately be reunited with our loved ones who have already transitioned? I know I am!

Amen! Amen! And Amen!

This concludes your final spiritual checkup.

Questions regarding your final checkup

1. Are you honest with God about your problems and weaknesses? Explain.

_____

_____

_____

2. Do you share your innermost thoughts with God, or do you somewhat hold back and share only the parts that you think only you understand? Explain.

_____

_____

_____

3. Are you truly giving Jesus your burdens and the cares of this world? Explain.

_____

_____

_____

My Life Experience in This Area

I remember a time in my life when it was extremely difficult for me to confess my problems and my weaknesses to God. It's not as if He didn't already know them anyway. I guess I thought God would think I was a failure. The Devil really has a field day in this area of our lives.

The hardest thing in this world for me to stop doing was cursing. I used to curse like a sailor. It was harder for me to stop cursing than it was for me to stop biting my nails, and I bit my nails up until I was about twenty years old. The Devil knew that cursing was one of my weaknesses. It was something that I strongly wanted to quit doing, yet the words just kept slipping out.

The reason that I say the Devil really has a field day with your weak points is because I would go a really long time without cursing and then one bad word would slip out and the Devil would cause me to feel like I wasn't saved. You see, the Devil plays with your mind. He wants you to give up and just say, "Forget it," and go back to your old ways.

Through God I was able to realize that once we confess our sins to God and ask for forgiveness in Jesus' name and request God's help in our areas of weakness, we grow stronger.

I don't care what your weaknesses or problems are. Be honest with God and call on Him for help. Your weakness may be lying, backstabbing, fornication, adultery, or something I haven't mentioned. If you fall, get back up. Don't allow the Devil to keep you in the mud for something that you used to do in the past. Along with God forgiving you, forgive yourself. When the Devil tries to remind you of your past, simply remind him that God has already forgiven you. Continue to stay strong in the Lord and be blessed!

What has the Holy Spirit shown me about confessing my weaknesses?

Journaling

_____

_____

_____

_____

_____

_____

_____

_____

_____

_____

_____

_____

Please turn the page for your spiritual diagnosis.

SPIRITUAL DIAGNOSIS

A CHRISTIAN IS SERIOUS ABOUT his or her spiritual walk and continues to strive for that perfection that will be attained when he or she meets with Jesus face-to-face. A Christian is committed to making the necessary changes that were identified during the series of spiritual checkups. Because the Christian has a personal relationship with God, he or she fully understands the significant role that prayer and study plays in this Christian journey. Overall, if the Christian continues to seek God's face, call on Jesus for help, and rely on the leadership of the Holy Spirit, spiritual success is inevitable.

—Minister Frances Knight-Pinckney

Road Map to Salvation

"THAT IF THOU SHALT CONFESS with thy mouth the Lord Jesus, and shalt believe in thine heart that God hath raised him from the dead, thou shalt be saved" (Romans 10:9).

If you have never accepted Jesus Christ as your personal Savior, please say the below *Prayer of Salvation* so that you can spend eternity in heaven when you leave this earth.

Prayer of Salvation for the Unsaved

FATHER GOD I ASK YOU to come into my heart and cleanse me. I admit that I am a sinner. I believe that Jesus Christ died on the cross for my sins. I believe that He rose on the third day with all power and is sitting on the right hand of You, making intercessions for me daily. Thank You, Father God, for saving me. In Jesus' name I pray.

Welcome to the Family of God

IF YOU SAID THE ABOVE prayer for the first time, I want to welcome you to the family of God. It's just that simple! *The angels in heaven are rejoicing right now just for you!* Find yourself a Bible-based church that preaches sound doctrine and teaches that Jesus is the Lord to help you on your new journey. Welcome my brother. Welcome my sister. Enjoy the journey!

APPENDIX

Scripture References (KJV)

The fear of the Lord is to hate evil: pride, and arrogancy, and the evil way, and the forward mouth, do I hate.

—Proverbs 8:13

No weapon that is formed against thee shall prosper; and every tongue that shall rise against thee in judgment thou shalt condemn.

—Isaiah 54:17

But ye are a chosen generation, a royal priesthood, an holy nation, a peculiar people; that ye should shew forth the praises of him who hath called you out of darkness into his marvelous light.

—1 Peter 2:9

Come unto me, all ye that labour and are heavy laden, and I will give you rest.

—Matthew 11:28

The thief cometh not, but for to steal, and to kill, and to destroy: I am come that they might have life, and that they might have it more abundantly.

—John 10:10

Ye are the salt of the earth: but if the salt have lost his savour, wherewith shall it be salted? It is thenceforth good for nothing, but to be cast out, and to be trodden under foot of men.

—Matthew 5:13

Be ye angry, and sin not: let not the sun go down upon your wrath.

—Ephesians 4:26

Be still, and know that I am God: I will be exalted among the heathen, I will be exalted in the earth. The Lord of hosts is with us; the God of Jacob is our refuge.

—Psalm 46:10–11

Now faith is the substance of things hoped for, the evidence of things not seen.

—Hebrews 11:1

Submit yourselves therefore to God. Resist the devil, and he will flee from you.

—James 4:7

For the ear trieth words, as the mouth tasteth meat.

—Job 34:3

Keep thy tongue from evil, and thy lips from speaking guile.

—Psalm 34:13

Death and life are in the power of the tongue: and they that love it shall eat the fruit thereof.

—Proverbs 18:21

And let us not be weary in well doing: for in due season we shall reap, if we faint not.

—Galatians 6:9

But seek ye first the kingdom of God, and his righteousness; and all these things shall be added unto you.

—Matthew 6:33

Greater is He that is in you, than he that is in the world.

—1 John 4:4b

For all the promises of God in him are yea, and in him Amen unto the glory of God by us.

—2 Corinthians 1:20

The light of the body is the eye: if therefore thine eye be single, thy whole body shall be full of light. But if thine eye be evil, thy whole body shall be full of darkness. If therefore the light that is in thee be darkness, how great is that darkness!

—Matthew 6:22–23

And we know that all things work together for good to them that love God, to them who are the called according to his purpose.

—Romans 8:28

It is written, Man shall not live by bread alone, but by every word that proceedeth out of the mouth of God.

—Matthew 4:4

In the world ye shall have tribulation: but be of good cheer; I have overcome the world.

—John 16:33

Thou hypocrite, first cast out the beam out of thine own eye: and then shalt thou see clearly to cast out the mote out of thy brother's eye.

—Matthew 7:5

Study to shew thyself approved unto God, a workman that needeth not be ashamed, rightly dividing the word of truth.

—2 Timothy 2:15

Seek, and ye shall find; knock, and it shall be opened unto you.

—Matthew 7:7

Take heed that ye do not your alms before men, to be seen of them: otherwise ye have no reward of your Father which is in heaven.

—Matthew 6:1

I have found David the son of Jesse, a man after mine own heart, which shall fulfil all my will.

—Acts 13:22

Keep thy heart with all diligence; for out of it are the issues of life.

—Proverbs 4:23

And he shall put the incense upon the fire before the Lord, that the cloud of the incense may cover the mercy seat that is upon the testimony, that he die not.

—Leviticus 16:13

I beseech you therefore, brethren, by the mercies of God, that ye present your bodies a living sacrifice, holy, acceptable unto God, which is your reasonable service.

—Romans 12:1

Now thanks be unto God, which always causes us to triumph in Christ, and maketh manifest the savour of his knowledge by us in every place.

—2 Corinthians 2:14

I have given them thy word; and the world hath hated them, because they are not of the world, even as I am not of the world.

—John 17:14

Love not the world, neither the things that are in the world. If any man love the world, the love of the Father is not in him. For all that is in the world, the lust of the flesh, and the lust of the eyes, and the pride of life, is not of the Father, but is of the world.

—1 John 2:15-16

When I was a child I spake as a child, I understood as a child, I thought as a child: But, when I became a man, I put away childish things.

—1 Corinthians 13:11

Let us lay aside every weight, and the sin which doth so easily beset us, and let us run with patience the race that is set before us.

—Hebrews 12:1

That it might be fulfilled which was spoken by Esaias the prophet, saying, Himself took our infirmities, and bare our sicknesses.

—Matthew 8:17

Therefore I take pleasure in infirmities, in reproaches, in necessities, in persecutions, in distresses for Christ's sake: for when I am weak, then am I strong.

—2 Corinthians 12:10

Weeping may endure for a night, but Joy cometh in the morning.

—Psalm 30:5b